EXTREME
SPORTS
No Limits!

Extreme
Surfing

John Crossingham & Bobbie Kalman

Crabtree Publishing Company

www.crabtreebooks.com

EXTREME SPORTS No Limits!

Created by Bobbie Kalman

Dedicated by Kelley MacAulay
For my parents, Susan and Bob, with all my love

Editor-in-Chief
Bobbie Kalman

Writing team
John Crossingham
Bobbie Kalman

Substantive editor
Niki Walker

Project editor
Kelley MacAulay

Editors
Molly Aloian
Amanda Bishop
Rebecca Sjonger
Kathryn Smithyman

Art director
Robert MacGregor

Computer design
Katherine Kantor
Michael Golka

Production coordinator
Heather Fitzpatrick

Photo researchers
Kelley MacAulay
Laura Hysert

Consultant
Paul West, President, United States Surfing Federation

Photographs and reproductions
AP/Wide World Photos: pages 7, 22, 26, 28
Image Select/Art Resource, NY: page 6
Jeff Divine: pages 4, 24, 25, 27
John Nordstrand: pages 5, 8, 9, 18-19, 20, 23, 29 (bottom), 30
B. Aroyan/Raw Talent Photo: page 3
B. Nevins/Raw Talent Photo: page 15
J. Nordstrand/Raw Talent Photo: pages 1, 14 (top), 21
Rich Reid/Colors of Nature: page 13 (middle)
Dave Homcy/Seapics.com: pages 12, 13
Other images by Corbis Images, PhotoDisc and Digital Stock

Illustrations
Katherine Kantor: page 28
Robert MacGregor: pages 10-11

Crabtree Publishing Company
www.crabtreebooks.com   1-800-387-7650

PMB 16A
350 Fifth Avenue
Suite 3308
New York, NY
10118

612 Welland Avenue
St. Catharines
Ontario
Canada
L2M 5V6

73 Lime Walk
Headington
Oxford
OX3 7AD
United Kingdom

Cataloging-in-Publication Data
Crossingham, John.
    Extreme surfing / John Crossingham & Bobbie Kalman.
      p. cm. -- (Extreme sports no limits series)
Includes an index.
Contents: Catching some waves--A Hawaiian tradition--Surfing takes off--Wave action--The boards--Surfing styles--Twisting and turning--Inside the tube--Up, up, and away!--Competitions--Legends of the surf--Today's surfing stars--A good start--Keep it safe.
    ISBN 0-7787-1669-4 (RLB) -- ISBN 0-7787-1715-1 (pbk.)
    1. Surfing--Juvenile literature. 2. Extreme sports--Juvenile literature. [1. Surfing. 2. Extreme sports.] I. Kalman, Bobbie. II. Title. III. Series.
    GV840.S8C76 2003
    797.3'2--dc22
                                                         2003016197
                                                         LC

CONTENTS

RIDE THE WAVE

Surfing is one of the world's oldest sports. It is an **individual sport**, which means athletes perform alone. Unlike many sports, surfing has no official rules. The basic goal is to **surf**, or ride ocean waves, while balancing on a **surfboard**. To make the sport more difficult, experienced surfers take on huge waves and do **tricks**, or moves, as they surf.

Surfing is known as an **extreme sport**. Extreme sports push athletes to the limits of their abilities. Many of the best surfers are **professionals** or "pros." They earn a living by surfing. Pro surfers often ride giant waves that can be very dangerous. They accept this risk. They enjoy the challenge of surfing the biggest waves and creating and mastering the most difficult tricks.

THE SURFER'S WORLD

Surfers have a unique **culture**. A culture is a set of values that a group of people shares. Surf culture is based on a love of riding ocean waves. The culture has its own music, fashion, and **lingo**, or way of talking. In the surfer's world, it is important to respect fellow surfers, especially older, more experienced riders. Above all, surfers respect the ocean, its wildlife, and its power. Surfers never forget that waves can be strong enough to injure or even drown careless riders.

USE EXTREME CAUTION

Surfing is a lot of fun, but it isn't easy. Do not attempt anything shown in this book. These surfers have practiced for years to master their sport. They are able to handle situations that are too dangerous for most people.

Not all surfers are human. Dolphins have also mastered this extreme sport.

A HAWAIIAN TRADITION

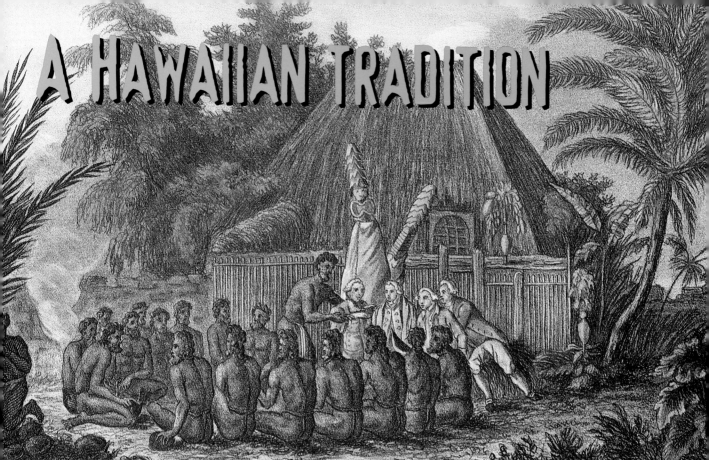

Many historians believe that surfing began thousands of years ago in **Polynesia**, a large group of islands in the Pacific Ocean that includes Hawaii. For ancient Hawaiians, surfing was part of their spiritual beliefs, culture, and daily lives. The **alii,** or Hawaiian chiefs, practiced surfing often. Their superior abilities helped prove their worth as leaders. They used two types of wooden boards—the **alaia** and the **olo**. People rode their boards lying on their bellies or standing up. The first Europeans to see surfing were Captain James Cook and his crew, who arrived in Hawaii in 1778. By the 1800s, European **missionaries** had arrived on the island. They tried to convince the Hawaiians to give up their religion and change their way of life. The missionaries banned surfing, and the sport nearly died.

Captain James Cook and his crew are greeted as they arrive in Polynesia.

BORN AGAIN

In the early 1900s, the surfing ban was lifted, and the sport's popularity slowly grew. A few surfing clubs were set up along Waikiki Beach, and friendly competition soon grew among them.

More and more young surfers started to practice the sport and challenge one another. American tourists in Hawaii quickly became interested in watching local surfers.

EXPORTING THE SPORT

Two of Hawaii's most famous surfers of the time helped spread the sport to other parts of the world. In 1907, George Freeth became the first pro surfer when he was hired to surf at Redondo Beach, California, to attract tourists. In 1912, Duke Kahanamoku began traveling to places such as California and Australia, where he inspired people to take up the sport. Kahanamoku is known today as the "father of modern surfing."

In 2002, the U.S. Postal Service created a stamp to honor the legendary Kahanamoku.

SURFIN' USA

At first, only a few Americans tried surfing because surfboards were very large and heavy. In 1926, however, a surfer named Tom Blake helped make boards more accessible—and surfing more popular—when he invented the first **hollow surfboard** (see page 11).

BETTER BOARDS

During the 1930s and 1940s, people experimented with other materials, making boards from balsa wood, **fiberglass**, and foam. In 1935, Blake improved surfboards again when he invented **skegs**, or fins that help keep boards from sliding out from under their riders (see pages 10-11). Skegs allow surfers to turn and pivot more sharply. With skegs, a whole new world of moves became possible, making the sport more exciting for both surfers and spectators.

Before the invention of skegs, a surfer turned the board by dragging one foot in the water.

THE GOLDEN YEARS

Surfing's popularity exploded in America in the 1950s. Movies and music featuring surfing became all the rage. Companies began manufacturing lighter, more affordable surfboards. With better boards, surfers became more daring.

THE SHORTBOARD REVOLUTION

In 1966, an Australian named Nat Young changed surfing forever when he used the first **shortboard** at a competition in San Diego, California. With his short, narrow board, Young made dazzling turns and graceful curves up and down the waves. He impressed judges and competitors alike. Surfers quickly gave up their old boards, which came to be known as **longboards**. By the 1970s, surfers everywhere were riding boards as short as six feet (1.8 m). Since that time, surfers have used shortboards to create increasingly radical moves which have earned surfing its reputation as an extreme sport.

*Longboarders often ride on the board's **nose**, or front end.*

MODERN SURFING TIME LINE:

1907: The first surfing club opens in Waikiki Beach
late 1930s: Companies begin mass-producing surfboards and experimenting with materials
1946: Preston Peterson builds the first fiberglass surfboard
1950s: Many famous companies, including Hobie, Hang Ten, and Jams, are formed; surf music and movies like Gidget *spark a surfing craze*
1960s: Corky Carroll becomes the world's first **endorsed**, or sponsored, pro surfer
1966: The movie The Endless Summer *inspires surfers to travel in search of new surf spots, helping spread the sport worldwide*
1973: Jack O'Neill invents the **leash** (see page 28)
1981: Surfboards with three skegs are introduced, giving surfers even more control over their boards
1990s: Longboards begin to make a comeback

THE BOARDS

Surfboards have come a long way from the heavy, solid wooden planks of the past. Today's boards usually have a **core**, or center, made of foam called **polyurethane**. The core is protected by a tough coating of fiberglass and **resin**. These materials make boards strong but lightweight.

THE LONG AND THE SHORT OF IT

There are two main types of surfboards—longboards and shortboards. Longboards are good for riding small, gentle waves. They are more stable and float better than shortboards do. Shortboards are easier to **maneuver**, so they are better for riding large, powerful waves. Besides length, a board's **outline**, or shape, also affects how it moves. A board with a curved outline turns more easily than one with a straight outline. Most surfers own many types of boards so that they can surf no matter what the waves are like.

THE LONG VERSION

Longboards are usually nine or ten feet (2.7 to 3 m) long. Their fairly straight outlines and rounded noses make them very stable. Surfers often move forward and backward to maneuver the boards and perform balancing tricks.

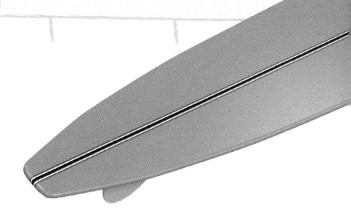

*To get a better grip, surfers rub **wax** on the decks of their boards. A grooved **traction pad** gives feet extra grip on the tails.*

deck

traction pad

tail

skegs

*All boards have between one and five skegs, which are also known as **thrusters**. Skegs make a board more maneuverable by keeping it from sliding sideways as it turns.*

*The sides of a board are called **rails**.*

nose

*The shape of a board's bottom surface is called the **bottom profile**. There are several bottom profiles, and each one creates a different ride. For example, a flat profile helps a board stay stable. A **concave profile** curves inward and makes the board easier to turn.*

THE SHORT VERSION

Shortboards are usually five to seven feet (1.5 to 2.1 m) long. They have curved outlines and pointed noses. Surfers shift their weight to maneuver these smaller, lighter boards. Shortboards are commonly used by pros because they are quick and easy to turn, making them ideal for tricks.

OVER THE YEARS

In the early days of surfing, boards had straight outlines and were very difficult to turn and control. Over time, designers created boards with different shapes, which allowed better control, sharper turns, and extreme riding.

Tom Blake's hollow board was based on the ancient Hawaiian olo. To make the board lighter, Blake drilled holes into it and then covered the board with a layer of thin wood to seal it.

*This **pintail outline** from the 1960s was faster and more maneuverable than any board before it. After speedy shortboards like this one became available, very few surfers wanted to ride longboards.*

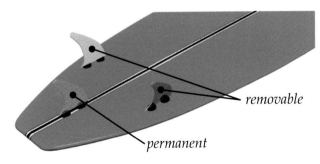

removable

permanent

*In the 1970s, the **tri-fin** was invented. This board had one permanent skeg and two removable skegs that surfers could position anywhere. This design gave surfers better control of their boards.*

11

WAVE ACTION

There are many types of waves, and each type provides surfers with different challenges. The wind, the ocean floor, and the shoreline all help determine the size and shape of waves in a particular location. The world's best places for surfing are Hawaii, Indonesia, and Australia's Gold Coast. These surfing spots have strong winds and the perfect land formations to create monster waves. California also has several famous surfing destinations, including San Diego, San Clemente, Santa Cruz, and Huntington Beach. Parts of Florida, North and South Carolina, and New Jersey also have good surfing conditions.

HOW WAVES FORM

Most waves are started by wind blowing across the water's surface. The stronger the wind blows, the faster the water moves. As the moving water approaches the shore, the ocean floor slopes upward and the wave is forced to slow down. There is less space for the wave under water, so the top of it gets pushed above the surface, where it forms a peak. As the wave nears the shore, the peak gets higher. Eventually, the wave grows so tall that its top falls over and **breaks**, or collapses.

*Waves often come in groups called **sets**, which provide surfers with consistent **swells**, or waves, to ride.*

GENTLE WAVES

The smallest waves that can be surfed are about two feet (0.6 m) high. They are called **non-breaking waves**, since they do not get tall enough to break. Surfers ride these waves just ahead of the **crest**, or the highest point of the wave.

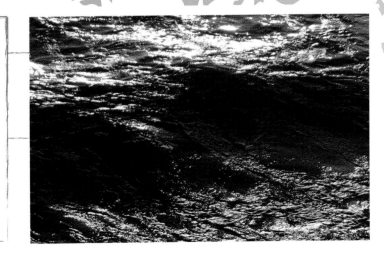

CATCH A BREAK

Breaking waves, or **breakers**, climb and form a curved wall of water before collapsing near the shore. Breakers can be two feet (0.6 m) to well over twenty feet (6.1 m) high! A surfer usually rides the pocket of a breaker, which is the fastest part. Surfers can also ride the lip.

A BARREL OF FUN

When a large wave hits a shallow bottom or **reef**, it breaks suddenly and forms a tunnel. This tunnel has many names—**tube**, **pipe**, **barrel**, **green room**, and **pit**. A tube lasts several seconds before it collapses. Surfers ride inside the tube, behind the wall of falling water.

CATCH A WAVE

The two main styles of surfing—
shortboarding and **longboarding**—
are named for the boards that are
used. Shortboard surfers make
swift, aggressive turns and perform
difficult tricks to **hot-dog**, or show
off, as they **cut** up, down, back, and
forth on waves. Longboard surfers
focus on balancing gracefully and
moving in tune with a wave.
Although their styles are different,
both shortboarders and longboarders
use the same basic techniques
while surfing.

*The ultimate longboard trick is the **hang ten**. A surfer
"walks the plank" to the nose and rides with all ten toes
hanging over it. Hanging ten requires an incredible sense
of balance and timing.*

PADDLE AND POP UP

Before surfers can ride the waves,
they first have to catch them. Most
surfers lie chest down on their
boards and paddle away from the
beach with their arms. They wait until
they catch a wave and then **pop up**.
In one quick motion, they grab the
rails, bring their feet underneath
them, and stand up on their boards.

*A smooth pop-up keeps the board balanced as the surfer
catches a wave.*

IN THE POCKET

Once they catch their waves, surfers rarely ride directly toward the shore. They move diagonally left or right, away from the breaking part of the wave. This way of riding is called **angling**. As they ride, surfers try to stay very close to the wave's pocket. To help keep their boards in the pocket, they use **leaning turns** to speed up or slow down. By leaning on either the left or the right rail, a surfer turns the board in that direction, making a wide, easy arc up or down the wave's face. This technique is also known as riding **rail-to-rail**.

Surfers perform leaning turns by shifting their weight from one rail to the other.

SURFER SPEAK

Surfers have come up with their own way of talking about their sport. Here are some common phrases:

Stance: *a surfer's body position on the board; a good stance has bent knees and legs wide apart*
Regular: *a stance with the left foot forward*
Goofy: *a stance with the right foot forward*
Carve: *to perform smooth turns along a wave*
Backside turn: *a turn that is done while the surfer's back faces the wave*
Frontside turn: *a turn that is done while the surfer's chest faces the wave*

Trim: *a surfer's position on the board in which he or she is not too far front, back, or to one side; proper trim allows for the fastest speed*
Wipeout: *a spectacular fall*
Bail: *to leap clear of the board during a wipeout*
Grommet: *a surfer under fourteen years of age*
Fan: *water that is sprayed in the air during a turn*
Air: *describing a situation in which a surfer's board is thrust up into the air, leaving the water completely*
Stoked: *describing a strong feeling of excitement or happiness*
Going ballistic: *surfing really well*

Leaning turns are great for smooth, easy cruising, but they are not very aggressive. Extreme surfing relies on faster, sharper turns known as **rear-foot turns**. A surfer makes this type of turn by pushing hard in one direction with the rear foot, using either the heel or the ball of the foot.

This sharp motion turns the board in the opposite direction. For example, pushing the rear foot to the left swings the nose of the board to the right. Rear-foot turns are a major part of shortboarding. These turns are possible on longboards, but swinging the long, heavy boards with one foot is difficult.

16

USING THE WHOLE WAVE

The pocket may have the most power, but pro shortboarders use the whole wave when they surf. They use a combination of leaning and rear-foot turns to maneuver their boards up, down, and back and forth across a wave's face.

TURN IT UP

The various turns that are used by shortboarders are named either for a surfer's body position or for the part of the wave on which the turn takes place. Here are some of the most common turns:

Bottom turn: a turn performed at the wave's *base*, or bottom, which a surfer uses to bring the board back up to the pocket

Off-the-lip: a term that describes a turn made at the wave's lip after riding up the face of a wave, which brings the surfer back down again

Layback: a turn that is done while the surfer leans as far back as possible; laybacks are often made at a wave's lip

Cutback or *slashback*: an aggressive rear-foot turn made at the end of a breaking wave, which immediately sends the surfer in the opposite direction

INSIDE THE TUBE

For both longboarders and shortboarders, riding in a tube is one of surfing's greatest challenges. It requires perfect control and timing. A surfer must remain balanced and stay just ahead of the collapsing part of the tube. Otherwise, he or she gets trapped in the wave and usually wipes out.

DUCK!

Sometimes, the waves are so large that they push paddling surfers back to the shore. To get past a large wave, a surfer **duck dives**, or pushes the nose of the board under the wave at just the right moment. The wave then passes over the surfer without pushing him or her back to shore.

DROPPING DOWN

When the right wave comes along, the surfer pops up and **drops down**, or rides over the lip of the wave and down its face. Dropping down gets the surfer into a good tube-riding position. The surfer then rides rail-to-rail and waits for the wave to break and form a tube just behind him or her.

The surfer often grabs the outside rail to gain extra control while crouching.

IN AND OUT

Once the tube forms, the surfer slows the board by pushing on the tail, which allows him or her to back into the tube. Inside the tube, the surfer crouches down. Staying low helps the surfer stay balanced and also speeds up the board again. If the board does not speed up, the surfer is swallowed by the wave! Skilled pros can also go **backdoor** into a tube— they come in behind the tube and surf forward into it.

UP, UP, AND AWAY!

Great surfers aren't limited to riding on water. The best can also fly through the air for brief moments! Surfers have to build up a lot of speed to shoot above a wave's lip and into the open air. In midair, they perform tricks called **aerials**, which have become more and more popular in the last ten years. Aerials are one of the most difficult surfing tricks. They are best suited to shortboards, although a few determined longboarders have also managed to get airborne. A basic aerial is performed by jumping off a wave and then successfully landing on the water. It might sound easy, but even a simple aerial is tough to master because a wave is always moving!

Many of today's surfing aerials started out as tricks invented on skateboards. Although surfboards aren't as maneuverable in the air as skateboards are, surfers still enjoy the challenge of trying skateboard-inspired aerials.

20

GET A HOLD OF IT

Surfers increase the difficulty of aerials by adding **grab tricks** to them. In a grab trick, the surfer grips part of the board while it is in the air. The surfer then has to move quickly to get back into a stance before landing. There are many types of grabs, and most have odd names. For example, the lien grab's name comes from "neil" spelled backwards. It's named after its inventor, skateboarder Neil Blender.

COMPETITIONS

The biggest test of a surfer's ability is competing against other surfers. Competitions are held for all ages and skill levels at beaches around the world. Surfers attempt to win by outdoing one another with their best tricks. Most pro events are for shortboard surfing, although longboard tournaments are becoming more popular.

THE ASP

Surfers enter their first competitions as **amateurs**. When they are ready to turn pro, they join the **Association of Surfing Professionals** (**ASP**). The ASP is the biggest pro-surfing organization. Every year it holds more than 50 events to determine men's and women's world champions in longboard and shortboard surfing. There are two levels of ASP competition: the **World Qualifying Series** (**WQS**), and the **World Championship Tour** (**WCT**). Surfers must do well in the WQS before they are allowed on the WCT.

One of the biggest competitions on the WCT is the Pipeline Masters in Hawaii. It takes place every December and is the tour's last event.

WHAT'S THE SCORE?

Competitors surf in groups called **heats**. Each heat has four competitors and lasts 20 to 30 minutes. Surfers catch as many waves as they can during their heat and perform a series of tricks as they ride each wave. Each surfer's performance is rated by five judges. Surfers' scores are based on their skills and the variety, difficulty, and speed of the tricks they perform. A surfer's two best rides are the only scores that count, so surfers hope to catch at least five amazing waves that will allow them to strut their stuff.

RACE FOR THE PRIZE

Besides enjoying the thrill of winning, the best surfers are well rewarded. Pros can make more than $100,000 for winning a single large event! They also earn money through **endorsements**, or deals that pay them to use or advertise a company's products.

Lip tricks are balancing moves performed on the lip of the wave.

Pros save their best moves for competitions. A full body spin, called a **360**, *is an aerial that few surfers can master.*

LEGENDS OF THE SURF

Since Duke Kahanamoku and George Freeth helped spread surfing's popularity around the world, many other men and women have also ridden waves into the history books. These pages show just a few of the surfing legends who helped shape the sport by challenging themselves and every wave they found.

DUKE KAHANAMOKU

Duke Kahanamoku is considered the father of modern surfing, and he was also an amazing swimmer—he broke the world record in the 100 meter freestyle event at the 1912 Olympics. He used his Olympic fame to spread the word about surfing from France to Australia. He even saved many lives by surfing out in heavy waves and rescuing people caught in storms!

TOM CARROLL

Tom Carroll, shown above, succeeded as a surfer despite his small size. Only 5'6" (168 cm) tall, this Australian surfer impressed everyone with his stocky strength and fearless riding from 1979 to 1993. Before Carroll, most top pros were tall men. He inspired shorter surfers to hit the waves. Despite many injuries during his pro career, Carroll won two world titles and numerous competitions.

KELLY SLATER

Florida native Kelly Slater is the best-known surfer in the world. At age 21, he became the youngest world champ ever. He has since won the ASP World Title six times! Slater has also appeared on TV shows, in magazine ads, and in movies. This well-spoken athlete even has his own surfing video game. Slater won the world title in 1998, and he still remains a top pro. He has brought more attention to the sport than any other surfer has.

TOM CURREN

California legend Tom Curren has surfing in his blood—his father was also a surfing champ. As a young kid, Curren was the best surfer America had seen in years. He spent the 1980s winning competition after competition, plus three world titles. During this time, he was the most popular surfer in the world. In the early 1990s, Curren left the pro tour. He traveled the world, filming his search for exciting new surfing locations.

LISA ANDERSON

Lisa Anderson is a Florida surfer who dominated women's competitions in the 1990s. She was the women's ASP world champion from 1993 to 1997. Only a few surfers, male or female, have ever won four world titles in a row! Anderson proved that women belong on boards and appeared in magazines that normally featured male surfers. Thanks to athletes like her, women's surfing is bigger than ever.

TODAY'S SURFING STARS

Every extreme sport needs young athletes to keep pushing its limits. Today's surfing pros are always finding ways to improve tricks and techniques. There are hundreds of great pros, but the surfers on these pages are some of the very best in the world. These amazing surfers constantly seek out more difficult tricks and more dangerous waves.

MARK OCCHILUPO

Mark "Occy" Occhilupo is an Australian star who has been a rival of Tom Curren and Kelly Slater for years. Although he was always a great surfer, in his early career he was unable to win a world title. Occy decided to leave pro surfing in the early 1990s. After working to get back in shape, he returned to the pro tour in 1995. He won the world title in 1999 and is still one of the best surfers in the world.

LAYNE BEACHLEY

Between 1998 and 2002, Layne Beachley, shown above, won the women's ASP title five times, breaking Lisa Anderson's record! In some years, the Sydney, Australia native has made more money than any other surfer, male or female. Beachley also gives back to her sport every chance she gets. She often acts as a guest commentator on sports programs and works hard to promote women's surfing.

CJ Hobgood

CJ Hobgood, shown right, is one of the best American surfers today. Born in 1979, Hobgood has surfed since he was six years old. His rise to fame has been fast. In 1999, he was the WCT rookie of the year, and in 2000, he was named the ASP's most-improved surfer. Just one year later, he became the men's world champion!

Dane Reynolds

For a few years, California's Dane Reynolds was considered the best amateur surfer in America. In 2003, Reynolds began competing in the WCT. Even though he has not yet proven himself as a pro, many experts think Reynolds could become the next Kelly Slater. Maybe he'll have his own video game someday!

Megan Abubo

Hawaii's Megan Abubo is one of the few serious challengers to Layne Beachley's throne. She has been ranked as high as number two in the world and continues to win worldwide competitions. She appeared as a body double in the surfing film *Blue Crush*.

KEEPING SAFE

Surfing can be a dangerous sport, but aside from a **wet suit** and a leash, surfers don't use any equipment. Instead of relying on padding to protect them, surfers rely on their knowledge of the waves to avoid bad wipeouts. They always follow the rules of the beach. Above all, surfers know how to swim! People who are not strong enough to swim at least 328 feet (100 m) in ocean waves should not even think about trying to surf.

WET WEAR

A wet suit is necessary for surfing in cold water. It is made of stretchy, tight-fitting rubber. The suit traps a thin layer of water against the skin. Body heat warms up this layer of water, helping the surfer stay warm and keeping cold water away from the surfer's body.

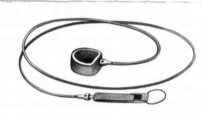

ON A LEASH

A surfboard is attached to a surfer's ankle with a leash. The leash prevents a surfer from losing his or her board in the water after a wipeout.

LOOK OUT BELOW

Many areas with good waves also have **scabs**—dangerous rocks on shore or just below the surface. During a wipeout, a wave can push a surfer onto these rocks and cause a serious injury. Before surfing at an unfamiliar beach, surfers check with the locals about any unsafe areas.

Surfers must be aware of dangerous areas to avoid.

FRIENDS FIRST

A group of surfers waiting for a wave is called a **line-up**. When in a line-up, a surfer should allow local or more experienced riders to go first. The surfer can learn a lot by watching them, and he or she will also earn their respect.

DON'T DROP IN!

In surfing, **dropping in** means trying to ride a wave that has already been taken by another surfer. Dropping in not only causes the risk of a nasty collision, but it's also bad manners! Nothing gets a young surfer booed off a beach faster than when he or she drops in on an experienced surfer.

Line-ups can be crowded. Surfers can avoid problems by respecting their fellow riders.

A GOOD START

After reading this book, you may want to grab a board and head for a beach. Before you hit the waves, it is important to be a good swimmer, have the right equipment, and an instructor to help you. Remember, the pros had to surf for years to become as good as they are now. Nothing in this book should be attempted by a beginner! The first step in becoming a surfer is finding a board. Top-of-the-line boards are very expensive, but inexpensive boards may not be well made. Ask an employee at a local surf shop for advice on which board is right for your body type and skill level. You may even find a great used board to buy from a local surfer.

Most pros recommend starting with a longboard. It will catch waves more easily and offer more stability and balance than a shortboard will.

TAKE IT EASY

When learning how to surf, take things slowly. Find a good coach who can answer questions and give you advice on your stance and technique. Never surf without your coach's supervision and approval. Beaches with shallow, non-breaking waves (see page 13) are the best places to learn basic skills like popping up and angling. Depending on where you live, you can also attend surfing camps.

EXTRA HELP

There are many ways to learn more about surfing. Magazines like *Surfer*, *Surfing*, and *Transworld Surf* all provide tips and product reviews as well as features on top pros. A lot of websites also have information on the sport. Finally, there are a number of great surfing movies that you can rent and watch at home. Whether they are silly or serious, they'll get you in the mood to carve some waves!

SURFING THE WEB

Plenty of websites offer information on surfing's history, stars, and equipment. Here are some sites where you can get started:

www.ussurf.org – official site of the United States Surfing Federation
www.surfart.com – plenty of surfing history and culture
www.aspworldtour.com – official site of the Association of Surfing Professionals
www.bbc.co.uk/wales/southwest/surfing – full of tips, glossaries, links, and more
www.qboards.com – a great place for tips when buying a new or used surfboard

GLOSSARY

Note: Boldfaced words that are defined in the book may not appear in the glossary.

alaia A nine-foot (2.7 m) long wooden surfboard used by ancient Hawaiians

amateur A person who loves to surf but does not earn a living doing it

cut To pass quickly across a wave

fiberglass A material made from very fine glass fibers

longboard A narrow surfboard, nine to ten feet (2.7-3 m) in length, that is ideal for beginners and for easy, relaxed surfing

maneuver To make a series of changes in direction

missionary A person who travels from place to place and tries to convert others to his or her religion

olo A seventeen-foot (5.2 m) long wooden surfboard used by ancient Hawaiians

professional An expert surfer who earns a living by competing in the sport

reef A ridge of rocks or coral that is close to the ocean's surface

resin A type of hard, smooth plastic

shortboard A rounded surfboard that is between five and seven feet (1.5-2.1 m) long, and which is ideal for aggressive riding

traction pad A large sticker with tiny ridges that is applied to the surface of a surfboard to give a surfer's foot better grip

tube The tunnel formed when a large wave suddenly collapses

wax A sticky substance that is applied to surfboards to give a surfer's foot better grip

INDEX

1 2 3 4 5 6 7 8 9 0   Printed in the U.S.A.   3 2 1 0 9 8 7 6 5 4